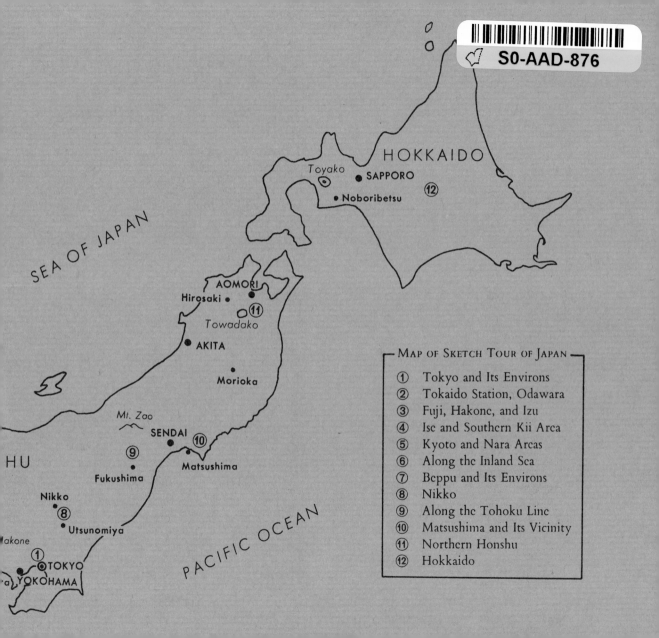

SEA OF JAPAN

HOKKAIDO

Toyako ● SAPPORO

● Noboribetsu ⑫

AOMORI

Hirosaki ● ⑪

Towadako

● AKITA

● Morioka

Mt. Zao

SENDAI ● ⑩

⑨

Fukushima ● ● Matsushima

PACIFIC OCEAN

HU

Nikko ●

⑧

● Utsunomiya

akone

① ⊙TOKYO

*a,*YOKOHAMA

S0-AAD-876

MAP OF SKETCH TOUR OF JAPAN

① Tokyo and Its Environs
② Tokaido Station, Odawara
③ Fuji, Hakone, and Izu
④ Ise and Southern Kii Area
⑤ Kyoto and Nara Areas
⑥ Along the Inland Sea
⑦ Beppu and Its Environs
⑧ Nikko
⑨ Along the Tohoku Line
⑩ Matsushima and Its Vicinity
⑪ Northern Honshu
⑫ Hokkaido

THROUGH JAPAN WITH BRUSH & INK

Chiura Obata

THROUGH JAPAN
WITH BRUSH & INK

CHARLES E. TUTTLE COMPANY
Rutland, Vermont & Tokyo, Japan

Representatives
For Continental Europe:
BOXERBOOKS, INC., *Zurich*
For the British Isles:
PRENTICE-HALL INTERNATIONAL, INC., *London*
For Australasia:
PAUL FLESCH & CO., PTY. LTD., *Melbourne*
For Canada:
M. G. HURTIG, LTD., *Edmonton*

Published by the Charles E. Tuttle Company, Inc.
of Rutland, Vermont & Tokyo, Japan
with editorial offices at
Suido 1-chome, 2–6, Bunkyo-ku, Tokyo

Copyright in Japan, 1968
by Charles E. Tuttle Co., Inc.

All rights reserved

Library of Congress Catalog Card No. 68–29545

First printing, 1968

PRINTED IN JAPAN

TABLE OF CONTENTS

INTRODUCTION

Throughout my life I have found great pleasure in trying to capture the beauty of natural and man-made creations with brush and ink, and during the past 75 years I have pursued my work with satisfaction. Early in my life, while under the tutelage of Moniwa Chikusen, master of the classical Tosa school of Japanese painting, I had the opportunity to visit important historical places in Japan with the old Japanese master painters.

Over the past several years I have accompanied various excursive groups from the United States on tours of these places. It is hoped that these simple brush-and-ink paintings may convey a fraction of the natural beauty radiating from Japan.

In trying to convey my impressions of the historic and scenic sites, I have attempted to paint the atmosphere with the customs that the people practice and the words they use. The name and description of a place, in translation, may not allow the image to be clear, so I have retained much of the commonly used Japanese terms. For example, Mt. Fuji is sometimes referred to as Fuji-san; Lake Biwa, as Biwako. In some cases, the reference to a place name such as Hakone, or Katsu-ura is the same for both English and Japanese. The following may serve as a guide to some of the Japanese terms used in the text:

hama: beach, shore	*shima; -jima:* island
hanto: peninsula	*seto:* channel, sound
jinja: shrine	*taki; -daki:* waterfall
kawa; -gawa: river, stream	*tera; -dera; -ji:* temple
ko: lake, lagoon	*ura:* inlet, harbor
saki; -zaki: cape, point	*wan:* bay
shi: city	*san; -zan; yama:* mountain, peak

In addition, when referring to person's names the Japanese form of surname first followed by the given name has been retained.

I am indebted to my old friend Wilder Bentley, associate professor of English, San Francisco State College, for polishing the English of my accompanying narrative commentaries, and also to Diana Wheeler, secretary of the English Department, for her assistance to him in the task of preparing the final copy.

CHIURA OBATA

SKETCH TOUR

§1. The Human Wave of Tokyo

Imagine this city of over ten million people, this capital city whose population accounts for more than a tenth of the Japanese nation. Everywhere one looks there is bustle and stir; every place a person walks he feels himself colliding with a tidal wave of humanity, whether in the Ginza, Asakusa, Ueno, Tokyo Station, Hibiya, or any other district of this megapolis. Then, too, one is aware of endless buildings rising toward the heavens. At such moments one feels as though he were hopelessly trapped by these waves of humanity between the endless man-made canyon walls; so much so that once he finds himself again in the open countryside where the old eternal modes of farming persist, it is as though he had been suddenly transported to another world remote from modern man.

§2. Visitors at the Imperial Palace Plaza

On longer acquaintance, however, after the visitor has became more used to the throngs of people everywhere on the streets of Tokyo, he becomes aware of individuals and types. For example, here at the Imperial Palace Plaza, he sees many groups of tourists, young and old, men and women, from all provinces and nations, arriving and departing every hour of the day. Then, too, there are those platoons of school children—boys and girls in their navy blue uniforms—parading around the plaza continuously. The tiniest of them have quaint yet practical tags sewed on their uniforms identifying them, in the event of a mishap, by name and school. Each flock seems shepherded by a teacher carrying a small pennant, apparently designed to keep his little troop in line and to avoid losing any of his wards.

§3. Asakusa Kannon Temple

Though all of Tokyo's ten million live in crowded quarters, the most teeming quarter of all is that surrounding the Asakusa Kannon Temple. In all the streets radiating from the temple's main entrance, one finds people closely packed together like sardines. In front of the temple there is a large wooden offering box into which the pilgrims drop their coins. Above this box a huge lantern hangs. A strange custom dating back to the Edo period still persists here, for on this lantern one sees inscribed the names of the leading geisha girls and geisha house owners.

§4. Kabuki Theater

Kabuki has come to epitomize the artistry as well as the magnificence of Japanese culture. It is no wonder then that the Kabuki Theater has been accepted as a rendezvous in the capital city for cultured people from all over Japan, as well as for distinguished visitors from abroad. During the performances given in this palatial theater, the audience senses all those spiritual qualities, those noble feelings that characterize the Japanese people at their best—a subtle blending of taste, tradition, and technique that enables this nation to give vent to its feelings without losing dignity and without sacrificing beauty.

§5. The Tokyo International House of Japan

A very important gathering place for foreign scholars and students, the Tokyo International House of Japan is located at Toriizaka, Azabu in Tokyo. In addition to housing lecture halls and halls for social affairs, it has facilities for boarding and lodging numbers of visitors from distant lands. Formerly the private estate of Baron Iwasaki, the grounds surrounding International House offer its visitors the comfort and delight of a beautifully laid out and carefully maintained Japanese garden in the great tradition.

§6. Night Scene on Ginza

All hues of neon lights flash in the night sky. Like dancers in the street, Ginza's endless streams of human souls move on and on. The walk is called *gimbura*, meaning without any set purpose or destination.

§7. Kamakura Beach

Along the undulating shoreline's length all the way from Odawara to Chiga-saki, Oiso, and Enoshima, the traveler is charmed by the sight of small boats wavering like sea birds along the sand dunes.

§8. Odawara Station on the Tokaido

How Hiroshige loved these pines! Pine trees were the bone and sinew of
"The Fifty-Three Stages of the Tokaido." Of endlessly fascinating forms and
shapes these pine trees are a source of wonder to the traveler. However, many
of them were felled during the Second World War for fuel, and we find
only here in this particular scene a portion of the grove in its original un-
spoiled state, very much as it must have looked in Hiroshige's time.

§9. Koki-an in the Rain

Koki-an in Odawara is one of the three famous teahouses built by the minister and art-lover, Yamagata Aritomo. His other two masterpieces, the Murin'an and Chinzanso, are in Kyoto and Tokyo respectively. Here at Koki-an what makes the traveler stand spellbound are the abundant waters sluicing down from the Hakone mountains in the background, plus a magnificent view of Sagami Bay to the east.

§10. Izu-Kawana

At one time the summer villa of the late Baron Okura, the Kawana Hotel stands in the midst of a great estate of several hundred acres, including two beautiful golf courses. Because of its mild climate, tempered by its Pacific coastline, plus the views of Hatsushima, Oshima, and other islands off its shores, one can almost imagine himself at Carmel with its Seventeen-Mile Drive, looking eastward over the mightiest of oceans.

§11. Izu Bay from the Fuji Observation Point at Hakone

Lying beyond tier upon tier of mountain ranges struggling to harmonize with the panorama, Izu Peninsula lies dreamily remote.

§12. Looking at Mt. Fuji from Daikanzan

Throughout the four seasons with their subtle changes of the scene one enjoys boundless views of Mt. Fuji whether he stays in one place or moves from vantage point to vantage point around its massive base. Among such endlessly pleasurable views, the one from Daikanzan (Mt. Daikan) is certainly the most dramatic. Before one lies Ashinoko (Lake Ashi) from whose distant shore rise rolling hills in a crescendo toward Fuji's very summit. By late afternoon, light deepens into shadow in the distance, while the few remaining clouds drift idly by leaving Fuji standing in the clear, calm evening sky.

§13. In the Gathering Dusk at Ashinoko

On his way to Ashinoko, after passing Jikkoku Toge (Jikkoku Pass) the traveler encounters this tranquil scene lying far below him in the evening calm.

§14. Mt. Fuji from Ashinoko, Hakone

The steep slopes around Ashinoko afford the viewer endless enjoyment because of their constantly changing shades and tints. Above and beyond them all towers Fuji in the distance like a prima donna surrounded by her chorus.

§15. Lakeshore at Ashinoko, Hakone

Wakasagi means pond smelt. Here we see a smelt fisherman's boat near the northern shore, rising and falling drowsily in the morning sun.

§16. The Torii of Hakone Shrine on Ashinoko

As the excursion boat nears Ashinoko's northern shore, Fuji grows ever more resplendent. The traveler marvels at the vermilion torii rising out of the Persian blue surface of the lake with a Japanese cedar grove serving as its backdrop.

§17. The Ferry Landing on Ashinoko

Within an hour ride from the Fujiya Hotel lie the deep blue waters of Ashinoko, the famous crater lake. Boarding a chartered ferryboat on its southern shore, one cruises northward and is treated to numerous views of Mt. Fuji above the distant hills. Then, when the eye becomes wearied by such grandeur, one can let his glances fall on shady places along the lake's shore, where mandarin ducks swim peacefully.

§18. Mt. Fuji at Daybreak from Owakidani

If you are once so fortunate as to see Mt. Fuji at dawn from Owakidani, then count yourself a lucky person, indeed! The following saying is proverbial in Japan. "If one be born under a lucky enough star he might just possibly experience a perfect view of Fuji." For our own part, the best we can say is that we have been trying. Year after year, rain or shine (and more usually the former), we have risen at dawn, hastily thrown on some clothes and rushed down to ask the desk clerk to telephone immediately the Hakone Hotel on the shores of Ashinoko in order to find out whether the weather conditions are to be propitious. *Miete kimashita!* comes the reply: "We can see it now!" We hire a taxi and head toward this beautiful vantage point at Owakidani, Hakone!

§19. The Bamboo Garden at Gora Museum, Hakone

About an hour's drive from the Fujiya Hotel at Hakone will take the traveler to the Gora Art museum, where he will find choice porcelains and other ceramic treasures from China and Japan of epochs past. The bamboo garden in front of the museum is renowned for its refreshing mists.

§20. Hakone Gorge

Like an artist-pilgrim of old visiting some ancient natural shrine, the traveler today feels refreshed in body and soul as he wonders at the lush green foliage of the trees growing on moss-covered black rock declivities and cliffs along Hakone gorge. Here not so much as a trail or trace of human habitation is to be seen!

§21. Miyanoshita Road from Fujiya Hotel, Hakone

At Miyanoshita is a familiar street scene very characteristic of those of hot spring resorts throughout Japan. The Fujiya Hotel was built over eighty years ago, and is a sister hotel to the Kanaya in Nikko. After a refreshing bath the traveler sips tea as he lets his eyes wander at random over the incongruous patterns of roof tops beneath his hotel window. There is something inimitable about this view that makes him well aware that he is in Japan.

§22. Grand Shrine of Ise

The path leading up to the shrine, Ise Jingu, is lined on both sides by ancient trees—Japanese cedar, pine, and *kusu* (Japanese camphor), being predominant. The traveler walks up this almost mile-long path listening to the soft crunching of pebbles beneath his shoes. Tranquillity prevails, and the visitor is awed by the divine beauty of this ancient place.

§23. The Five-Colored Rooster of Ise Shrine

According to legend, the Goddess Amaterasu is said to have secluded herself in a rocky cave. Prince Ame-no-Uzume performed a bell dance in front of the cave in an effort to lure the goddess out, yet without success. Finally he had a cock brought to the mouth of the cave whose crowing so entranced the goddess that she came out of seclusion. To commemorate this legend the great Shrine of Ise was erected, and as a result the five-colored cock itself has become a sacred symbol.

§24. The Grand View of Ago Bay from Shima Kanko Hotel

The late Mikimoto was the grand old man responsible for having started the now flourishing cultured pearl industry of Japan here on beautiful Ago Bay. Every island in the bay is heavily wooded with green pines the year round, with cherry blooms in spring, azaleas in summer, and many-hued maple leaves in the fall. Beneath these trees and shrubs an abundance of wild flowers add their hues and forms to this natural tapestry. One of the unusual features of this region is the great number of bush warblers whose song can be heard throughout spring. Fresh sea breezes sweep in from blue expanses revealing island after island out to the horizon's very brim.

§25. The Pearl Rafts on Ago Bay

The guest is awakened from his dreams as the throbbings of a trawler motor come through the open bedroom window. Gazing out over the bay, the distant pearl rafts can be seen rising and falling among the islands in the early morning light. In the clear blue sky a gull's wings flash and gleam as they slowly cleave their way. While far below the fishermen are busied with their morning tasks, making ready their fleet of tiny boats before they set out for the day's catch.

§26. The Shipwrights of Anori

After about an hour drive in a northwesterly direction from the Shima Kanko Hotel, the traveler comes upon the fishing village of Anori, situated on an arm of the shoreline that encloses the bay of that name. On the beach, still wet from flood tide, three or four shipwrights are earnestly at work constructing a thirty-five foot fishing boat. They are using the same hand-forged tools as their forefathers. I ask, "How much does a boat like this one cost to make?" "Oh, about one hundred dollars in American money," one of them replies. Just think of it! And for all that handwork!

§27. The Violent Surf at Nagiri

At the southeastern tip of Shima Peninsula, lies the little fishing village of Nagiri. Great combers come crashing in against its headland cliffs of weathered basalt. As each billow buffets and retreats, one hears the roar and hiss of shingle sucked out by the tide. On every rocky promontory's summit cling ancient pines, their branches swaying in the spume and spray. Truly, places like Nagiri have ever been, must always be, the favorite haunts of artists.

§28. The Nachi Falls

Four hours by train from Osaka to Katsu-ura Station and from there another forty minutes by bus brings the traveler to the famous Nachi Falls, highest in Japan. Stone steps fashioned in the Kamakura period lead down to the foot of the falls through a grove of Kumano cedars where one passes through a great torii such as those found at all Shinto shrines. Here young and old crowd together to marvel at the falls as they recall the old romance of the saintly Mongaku.

§29. The Natural Bridge at Kushimoto

At Kushimoto Beach near Katsu-ura Harbor, rocks arch out from the beach to an island offshore, thus forming a natural bridge. People call it Hashikui-iwa.

§30. A Grand View of Katsu-ura, Nanki

The Kumano Express leaves Osaka at half-past nine in the morning, and arrives at Katsu-ura Station about three in the afternoon. Here the traveler transfers to a local bus and arrives at Katsu-ura Harbor a short while later. Deep Katsu-ura Bay lies toward the east, with its magnificent scenery and fleets of fishing boats resting at anchor. Crossing the bay by ferry the traveler reaches the island of Katsu-ura where he is welcomed by maids from the Katsuraso Hotel. Dressed in traditional kimono they guide all the newly arrived guests of the hotel through a natural tunnel. A grand view awaits each guest at the tunnel's exit; the hotel proper is cantilevered from the tunnel's mouth far out over the Pacific Ocean.

§31. Fishing Village at Katsu-ura

From a hill behind the Katsuraso Hotel one looks down upon a peaceful
fishing village—peaceful at this season of the year at least. The large trawlers
seen resting at anchor are bonito boats which range over the South Seas during the height of the fishing season.

§32. Sandan-heki, Nanki

A half-hour drive from Shirahama, the famous Sandan-heki (Sandan Cliff) towers several hundred feet above the Pacific. In windy weather the combers strike this cliff with such violence that one can become dizzy standing near its brink amid the roar. Here people disport themselves by sailing clay plates, sold at a nearby shop, out over the vast ocean from the cliff's edge. The plates soar and dip like swallows in flight until at last they plummet into the abyss.

§33. Shirahama Senjojiki

Senjojiki (meaning an area large enough to require one thousand *tatami,* or grass mats, to cover it) is well named. As a picnic ground it easily accommodates several hundred people. And with its magnificent view of brown and golden ocher stone from the top of Shirahama Cliff, it is a most popular spot for picnickers.

§34. View of Kyoto from the Miyako Hotel

Kyoto, the mecca of Japan, is famed for its thirteen hundred temples and three hundred shrines. It still retains much of its ancient glory as Japan's first great capital. The guest staying at the Miyako, oldest European-style hotel in the city, is fascinated during the breakfast hour by his panoramic view of this lovely city mellowed by age and softened in outline by countless tree-lined streets. Through the mist of an early autumn morning the roof of Nanzenji (Nanzen Temple) is seen looming above the ancient pines, while in the far distance the contours of Mt. Hiei are descried.

§35. Saihoji

Saihoji (Saiho Temple commonly known as "The Moss Temple") is situated on the western outskirts of Kyoto. Founded by Prince Shotoku and Gyoki, it is of great antiquity. About six hundred years ago the temple was restored and its garden landscaped in the Kamakura period style by Priest Muso. The teahouse, called Shoman-tei, is one of Japan's national treasures, while on a neighboring hillside slope is a famous *karetaki,* or "dry waterfall." Once inside the temple gate, the visitor senses the delightfully soothing peacefulness of the place as he examines the soft hues and textures of the many different varieties of moss covering virtually every inch of the garden.

§36. The Rock Garden of Ryoanji

One of the most diverting pastimes of travelers is to visit some of the more famous rock gardens of Kyoto and compare their subtle charms. Especially noteworthy are those at Ryoanji (Ryoan Temple), Katsura Rikyu or Katsura Detached Palace, Kinkakuji, Sambo-in, and Saihoji. In these five masterpieces of the landscape gardener's art (an art combining many artistic disciplines into one) one finds the ultimate in austerity and simplicity.

§37. The Water Basin in the Courtyard of Ryoanji

In the courtyard of the ceremonial tearoom of Ryoanji our attention focuses
on its water basin. We admire its beautiful natural contours. Engraved on the
basin is a four character motto: *Ware tada taru-o shiru*, meaning: "I know
only satisfaction." For what is more refreshing than tea steeped in pure
spring water?

§38. Sekisui-in at the Great Kozanji in Togano-o

Kozanji (Kozan Temple) in Togano-o, as the northern section of Kyoto is called, is a famous example of Zen austerity in temple design. It was established in the early Kamakura period by Myoe Shonin. Here the only sound heard is the muted rippling of the Kiyotaki River as it flows through the grove of huge *kaede* maple trees nearby. In the temple proper are preserved the famous sketches done by the one-time resident priest, Toba Sojo. To the rear of the temple are the remnants of the original tea trees imported from China long ago. History books tell us that Kenrei Mon' in, the widowed mother of the child emperor, Antoku, visited Myoe Shonin here and became a nun. We are not told how this remarkable woman managed to save her own life and that of her son by hurling herself and her child into the sea following the defeat of the Taira clan by the Genji clan at the Battle of Dan-no-ura over nine centuries ago; yet this heroic feat she somehow accomplished, if we are to believe documentary accounts.

§39. A Maple-Viewing Party at Kiyotaki River

Over a thousand years have passed since Kyoto was first designated as the capital of Japan. Yet even so the Kyoto spirit still pervades this impressive city. Its people still revere its past magnificence by their devotion to the maintenance of its monuments and shrines which they themselves still visit, enjoying the seasons of the year among its groves and gardens. For example, in this sketch we see groups enjoying the autumn colors along the banks of the Kiyotaki River with the *kaede* maples at the peak of their beauty.

§40. A Grove of Maples at Takao

This sketch shows an especially beautiful grove of *kaede* maples (a variety of large leaf maples peculiar to this region) at Takao lying somewhat to the north of the ancient capital. The traveler can become lost in the crowd of admiring visitors among these great trees. Wherever he looks there are still more great arching boughs of flaming gold and crimson!

§41. On Excursion down the Honzu River Rapids

In the accompanying six sketches we are given an artist's first-hand impressions of a thrilling experience, that of shooting the Hozu River rapids. The excursionist finds himself seated in a specially designed flat-bottomed boat, thirty-five feet from stem to stern, with a five-foot beam. Each craft is manned by a bowman, an oarsman, and a helmsman. The bowman stands close behind the prow and wards off dangerous rocks and snags with his twenty-foot bamboo pole as the boat shoots the rapids, down the narrow rocky gorges. Seated just in front of the passengers, the oarsman with quick deft strokes keeps the boat on an even keel. Standing far astern, the helmsman, the veteran of the crew, steers the boat by means of a large scull which he handles in perfect coordination with the efforts of the other two crewmen. It is remarkable to note that these seasoned oarsmen are actually farmers who live near the village of Kameyama and till the soil during the farming season. It is only during the tourist season—March, April, May in the spring, and August, September, October in the fall—that they take to boats in order to shoot the Hozu rapids for our benefit.

We board the boat at Kameyama, and soon we are shooting down the gorge. Like an endless motion picture on either side of us, scene after scene sweeps by, as wooded slopes covered with Japanese cedars, pines, zelkovas, chestnuts, cherries, maples, and camelias follow one another in rapid succession. The cherry blossoms of spring are most effectively displayed in such a dramatic setting as this, with their riotous pinks erupting out of the sylvan greens. In the autumn Hozu gorge becomes a virtual fireworks display with its wild outbursts of yellows, browns, vermilions, and crimsons of maples set off by the great sculptured forms of jutting rocks. Indeed, the traveler finds many landscapes here that recall the painting of the master Sesshu as well as the lesser masters of the Kano, Tosa, and Shijo schools. It is thanks to such artists as these that Kyoto has so many famous landscape gardens; yet even so, these same artists received much of their inspiration from these views that we encounter along the Hozu River.

As though to cap the climax of our two-hour excursion, we come to rest at the Rankyo Inn, situated on a rocky ledge on the river's right bank. And as we settle down to enjoy our evening repast in the large dining hall, a shoji screen is opened so that we can look down through the limpid air where a soft breeze ripples the river's edge—the same breeze that is apt to waft a stray cherry blossom or a gold-and-red maple leaf into the hall where it comes to rest like a celestial gift on one of our dinner trays.

§42. A Feast in the Junidanya Restaurant

Tucked away in a corner of Kyoto's Gion quarter, is an unpretentious little restaurant which is as famous for its cooking as for its antiquity. This tiny building has but three *zashiki* (guest rooms), so that it can accommodate only thirty diners at a time, yet it has been constantly patronized for the past several hundred years. The secret of its popularity lies in its gourmet's speciality—*mizutaki* (water-boiled) cooking.

All cooking is done in front of its guests in a special cast-iron charcoal boiler from whose top protrudes a chimney. When the soup stock starts simmering, sliced pieces of beef are placed in the broth. The beef cooks instantly. After dipping the pieces of beef into a special sauce made of *shoyu* (soy sauce), sesame seeds, kelp, bonito flakes, and hot pepper, each diner consumes his portion of meat with relish, for the Tajima beef, as it is called, virtually melts in one's mouth! Following this course, each guest now puts the fresh vegetables on his plate into the boiler. Then, as a last course, the soup stock itself, greatly enriched by new juices from the cooking, is poured over the bowl of rice provided each guest for this purpose. Mr. Nishizaki, the restaurateur, and his wife, both clad in spotlessly white aprons, see to it that each guest experiences a gourmet's satisfaction at this dining place. To add to the zest of the repast the walls of each room have been skillfully decorated with appropriate specimens of the best folk art.

§43. Sarusawa Pond, Nara

Older even than Kyoto, Nara has stood on its ancient site for the past thirteen centuries. In this sketch we enjoy one of the most celebrated views of this city as we gaze across Sarusawa Pond toward the magnificent proportions of the five-storied pagoda of Kofukuji (Kofuku Temple). Here time stands still, while through the soft spring rain we watch the cherry petals float beneath the overhanging fresh green wands of a pond-side willow tree, just as they have done since the beginning of time. One thinks of *Man'yoshu,* the collection of earliest Japanese poems.

§44. Kasuga Shrine, Nara

Every temple, every pagoda, every gate in Nara has the indelible marks of age upon it, save one exception. For here we find the brilliantly resplendent vermilion of the torii to the famous shrine of Kasuga Jinja, as well as the main entrance, ceremonial hall, treasure house, and surrounding fence. Suspended from the beams of the temple are hundreds of bronze lanterns donated three or four hundred years ago by worshipers. An aged Japanese cedar tree grows in the ceremonial courtyard. Muted by its dense, bluish green foliage, the airs of ancient tunes played by two men in Heian period costumes solemnly rise. Maidens perform the sacred dance known as *kagura* which seems appropriate in such a setting.

§45. The Sacred Deer of Nara

In the nearby Nara Park, many hundreds of deer roam at large. They are protected and revered as sacred messengers to the Kasuga Jinja. All of them are quite tame, so tame in fact, they are apt to follow visitors about, expecting to be fed; in turn, they are supposed to give comfort to their benefactors.

§46. Horyuji

From the village of Ikaruga a pathway down a pine-lined avenue leads the visitor toward the oldest wooden structure in the world, built in the seventh century A.D. As he approaches the main gateway to Horyuji (Horyu Temple), he notices a long earthen wall stretching far to the east and west of the entrance. Both its weathered contours and its color give one the impression that it must be thousands of years old. Then as the visitor looks through the gateway into the temple courtyard, he sees the real beauty of simplicity in the use of natural materials. From whatever angle one views the structure, whether as a whole or in detail, one has the feeling of viewing works of art. All such works fusing into one work of art—the ultimate in temple structure!

§47. The Ancient Wall in Horyuji

In ancient times Horyuji was first built on the far eastern side of Chuguji
(meaning "Nun's Temple") which was the main structure. Forty-eight
temples in all were completed, but due to the ravages of time most of them
have long since been destroyed. As mute evidence of their one-time grandeur only this earthen wall, its coping of blue tile almost completely
covered with moss, still survives. Yet here and there an aged pine, zelkova,
maple, or cherry tree, splashing the landscape with its seasonal hues, still
serves as a memento to impress the visitor.

§48. The Oyster Beds on Hiroshima Bay

A large part of the annual oyster production of Japan is concentrated in the great beds that lie offshore around the city of Hiroshima. In the sketch we see a characteristic stretch of Hiroshima Bay and coastline with its old wind-sculptured pines clinging to rocky promontories. On the bay's surface in the distance a typical *sudate* (a floating oyster bed made of bamboo lattice-work) makes an attractive screenlike design on the water. In the midst of this trellis-like raft, as though to give it interest as well as scale, we observe an oysterman cleansing young oysters that cling to ropes suspended from the bamboo trellis which can be raised or lowered at will.

§49. The Frontal View of Itsukushima Shrine

Over nine centuries ago the Genji and Heiki clans clashed in a desperate struggle for political power. In the resultant strife the Heiki clan was defeated, and their great palace, Rokuhara, was reduced to ashes. Yet by some miracle their shrine, Itsukushima, was never molested then or during the ensuing years. Thus the traveler is able to recapture some of the glory of ancient Japanese aquatic architecture, unequaled in its ability to harmonize land and water through the buoyancy of wood.

§50. View Through Spring Rain at Itsukushima

In this sketch we view from another aspect the floating shrine, built as a petitionary offering by Taira no Kiyomori. As we look across the water through a light drizzle we see a vermilion reflection from this torii swelling toward us on each successive undulation. What an awe-inspiring union of land and sea—while far in the distance lies deep blue Misen (mountain) to complete this classical landscape!

§51. The Pilgrims from the Ferryboat

Joining the travelers disembarking from the ferryboat to Itsukushima, we walk among the teeming hordes of people along the waterfront passage. Such scenes are typical of Kyoto or Nikko or Nara, since everywhere one looks the streets are lined with souvenir stores, many of them selling the same merchandise. We wonder how they can all stay in business!

§52. In the Memorial Park at Hiroshima

We look across the river toward the ruins of Hiroshima and toward the new park and monument dedicated to the atomic bomb victims. Marking the epicenter of this man-made holocaust, stands a huge horseshoe-shaped casket styled after the Jomon period. The arch serves as a frame for the distant view of the remaining ruins of Shoko Shoreikan. Directly beneath the arch has been set a granite stone on which is inscribed: "Pray rest in peace, and never repeat such a tragic blunder!" Under this monument the names of over one hundred thousand victims of the bomb lie buried.

安らかに
眠って下さい

過ちは
繰り
返しませぬから

§53. Inland Sea Landscape

In this sketch we can enjoy a typical scene along the coast of Seto Naikai (Inland Sea of Seto). Islands and islets of manifold shapes covered with dense foliage, dot the sea's surface, resembling miniature counterparts in some school of landscape gardening. Fishing boats ride the gentle swells like sea gulls resting their wings.

§54. A View of Beppu Bay

Both Osaka and Kobe, flourishing industrial cities and ports on the Inland Sea, are served by rail and water routes. However, most travelers prefer the approach by water because of the many beautiful stretches of coastline on both sides of the Inland Sea. In fact, while cutting through the white caps in Bungo Suido (Bungo Channel) the traveler can see both shores at once. On the left shore he sees the great chimney stack of the copper smeltery of Saganoseki. On the right, lies a coastline very similar in contours to that near San Simeon, California. The city of Beppu can be clearly seen farther to the left with hills and mountains serving as backdrop.

Covered with oddly shaped green trees resembling cupcakes, the mountains behind Beppu are the haunts of the wild monkeys for which this region is renowned. About a half-hour drive from the city brings one to their domain. Since about 1952 these monkeys have been the wards of the monks of the Zen temple which owns and controls all this mountain sanctuary. Under such benign wardenship the number of wild monkeys has increased rather than decreased over the years, the present population totaling some six hundred. Over one hundred stone stairs lead to the crest of their mountain from which one may·view many monkeys on the ground among the trunks of trees. Far above—sometimes on a topmost crag or on a lofty treetop branch—a lookout monkey keeps constant vigil to alert the others in the event of danger. In comparison to human society, these monkeys live in a peaceful community.

§55. A View of Mt. Takasaki

Suginoi Onsen (a hotel and hot spring resort) on Kankaiji Hill at Beppu, is renowned for its beautiful view, its clean and comfortable rooms, and its excellent handmaids. Mt. Takasaki may be seen simply by opening the shoji of one's bedroom. In front of the hotel is a charming garden among pine trees and *moso* (Phyllostachys) bamboo, while in the far distance lies the Inland Sea, to add that stroke of cool, blue water that characterizes classical Oriental landscape art.

§ 56. Old Japanese Cedar in the Compound of Toshogu, Nikko

"Never say *kekko* (magnificent) until you've seen Nikko!" runs the old saw. And, indeed, the traveler even after many visits is always taken aback by the magnificence of its architecture, especially by that of the Toshogu (shrine). Under the Tokugawa shogunate great feudal daimyo (lords), vied with one another to see who could contribute the most money and labor in order to construct this great shrine and provide the elaborate altar appointments and other ritualistic treasures that are lavished on such sacred places of worship. But most impressive of all such acts of reverence was that of Matsudaira Masatsuna, Lord of Kawagoe, to whom we should be ever grateful for donating and tastefully planting the Japanese cedar trees that surround the temple complex. It is these natural appointments that give the shrine its atmosphere of unified and harmonious distinction. Without the softening effect of their foliage, the gaudiness of the Tokugawa style, almost as unrestrained as Portuguese baroque, would be overwhelming! It is largely the muting effect of these ancient trees that makes Nikko what it is today.

§57. Nikko Shrine in the Rain

Despite the Japanese cedar's subduing effect it is true that the architecture of Nikko, painted in gold, silver, and brilliant primary colors and decorated with elaborate engravings and sculptures, is very tiring to the eyes in brilliant sunlight. The seasoned visitor prefers inclement weather, particularly a day of quiet misty rain for the viewing. Under the deep shade of the gigantic trees a cluster of Japanese umbrellas, shielding visitors to the shrine, move like bubbles on a densely shaded pool of water.

§58. The Changing Mists of Nantaizan

Nantaizan (Mt. Nantai) rises majestically above her bed of clouds to reveal her verdant beauty washed and refreshed after a recent shower. Below, the clouds dispersing into serpentine mists glide down her lovely water course, the Daiyagawa (Daiya River), and envelop the other hills and valleys beneath her summit.

§59. Kegon Waterfall, Nikko

The clear water of Chuzenjiko (Lake Chuzenji) descends over three hundred feet in the famed Kegonnotaki (Kegon Falls). A natural formation of volcanic rock of a deep blackish brown color juts far out from both sides at the top of the falls resulting in a thunderous tumult, as the great masses of water crash down and disappear into a cloud of mist and spray at the base. To add to the drama of the scene, colored maple trees cling precariously to narrow ledges on both sides of the falls. For the best view the visitor should take the elevator down three hundred feet to the viewing platform close to the falls' basin. From there wild cascades vanish into a winding gorge on their way toward a mysterious, unknown world below.

In Nikko National Park, besides this waterfall, there are the Shirakumo, Kirifuri, and Urami Falls.

§60. Remnants of Snow at Chuzenji in Nikko

In some years snow falls at Nikko as late as the latter part of March. Here we see the shores of Chuzenjiko still covered in mid-March with two-to-three feet of snow. Standing amid this white brilliance is Chuzenji's main hall, shining beautifully in pure vermilion.

§61. Early Spring on Chuzenjiko

Here again is Chuzenjiko this time as the warm rays of an early spring sun are calling forth the buds in the trees, while the snow has retreated to the tops of distant mountains. Yet the lake still slumbers on in a deep hibernal sleep.

§62. Shirakumo Falls

Somewhat to the left of Kegon Falls, the traveler suddenly encounters a magnificent view of Shirakumo (White Cloud) Falls cascading down its seriate tiers of solid stone.

§63. Mt. Zao

En route from Tokyo north to Sendai the traveler passes through Utsuno-miya, Shirakawa, Fukushima, until at last, as a sign that he is approaching his destination, Mt. Zao lies to the left, still capped with snow. Since winter is almost gone, patches of yellow and pink can be seen here and there over the fields and mountains. Yet the breeze is still keen with winter's chill.

§64. Two Studies of Peasant Passengers

Peddlers with their heavy burdens of marine products, both fresh and dried, board the train and come rushing into the day coach to find seats. Already tired, though it is early morning, the women rest quietly without forgetting their manners, whereas the men lie sprawled in their seats, trying to grab a wink of sleep.

§65. A Primitive Saw Pit and Carpenter's Shop

With a two-handed saw and crosscut, plus axes, adzes, and other tools of the trade, this primitive mountain woodshop is open to the weather on three sides with only the west side sheltered by a crude wooden wall. Cold winds sweep freely through this drafty shed. There are no fixed hours of labor here where the eight-hour day was never heard of! From break of day until dark of evening, its owner and operator times his activities like those of the birds! When I inquired of the owner, "How's business?" He replied without irony, "I have been doing this for the past thirty years, and I have not saved so much as a yen. But, you see, I like to operate this little shop because here on my mountainside the river runs so very near."

§66. A Mountain Village in Tohoku

This mountain village seems to grow where and how it will, like the surrounding wild shrubs and trees. Houses, shops, sheds, and all the rest seem like random growths; like weeds in a field gone fallow. Yet there is an organic unity and harmony about it all that one misses in cities. Even the handmade banners and signs seem to belong to a natural order much older than mankind.

§67. A Farmer's Folkcraft

Strangely enough, it is believed that the so-called *kokeshi* dolls, at present so popular in the United States as well as in Japan, originated in the small farming community adjacent to the Narugo Hot Springs in Miyagi Prefecture. It appears that the making of the dolls began as a pin-money folkcraft among the farmers of Togatta during the slack season. Here we see a typical roadside scene of this region, with *mizuki* wood piled neatly in front of an ideally designed farmhouse at a bend in this quiet mountain road. The wood is being seasoned preparatory to being fashioned into *kokeshi* dolls during the winter months.

§68. Village Children at Play

Unlike American children playing cowboys and Indians in full regalia including pistols and bows, the Japanese children in this country town can afford only sticks as playthings. Yet they seem healthy and happy enough, despite playing in the dusty open country road as a cold wind blows down from Mt. Zao to the west.

§69. A Country Woman with Her Burden

Snow-capped Zao is seen in the distance, across fields of dried *susuki* (pampas grass). Country girls carrying large bundles of *daikon* (radish) weighing from seventy to eighty pounds are a common sight.

§70. "Daikon" Harvest

As heavy frost is forming on the *daikon* field, a farmer and his wife, aided by two young girls, toil under the clear autumnal skies of early morning. The wife is saying, "We started sowing so late this year that I feared the yield would not be good, but the crops have grown very well, indeed!" The husband replies, "Yes, they have grown well, haven't they? How many do you think we ought to pickle—five or six hundred, say?" In such a peaceful serenity as this natural scene offers plain speech becomes pure poetry!

§71. Villagers Repairing a Road

In Japan, particularly in the villages of the northeastern region, the people must face a long winter without any income. Naturally such people live at a great disadvantage compared to those living in the warmer southlands, where food is more plentiful and fuel is less of a necessity. As a result, most northern mountain villagers live in a state of poverty often bordering on destitution. Since there are no tax funds available for the maintenance of roads, the roads must be repaired by volunteers from each household—men and women alike work mending them with nothing but hard luck for pay.

§72. A Public Bathhouse

About a two-hour drive south of Sendai the traveler enters a canyon famous for its autumn display of many-hued maple trees. The effect is enhanced by the crystaline clear Shiroishi River mirroring back many riotous colors from its swirls and eddies. In an especially beautiful scene, the river bends around a rocky point on which a public bathhouse has been constructed by the local village folk, for the use of themselves as well as any visitors to this place.

§73. Sacred Dancing, Shiogama Shrine

Shiogama Shrine was erected over a thousand years ago as the spiritual guardian and sanctuary of northeastern Japan. Built on a hillside overlooking the large fishing port of Shiogama, the shrine looks southward over the city in the distance with a panoramic view of Matsushima Bay beyond. The shrine is frequented by local fishermen praying for a better catch and for protection from the hazards of the sea, as well as by expectant mothers hoping for a safe delivery. In the accompanying sketch we see vestal virgins performing the *kagura,* or sacred ritual dance, that aids petitioners in the birth throes.

§74. A Glimpse of the Sea Through Pine Boughs

Connected with the center of Matsushima Park by a long wooden bridge, Fuku-urashima lies within easy walking distance. On this island a bridge tea-house has been provided to offer visitors charming vistas of the nearby trees of many species as well as glimpses of the sea. In this sketch we catch a characteristic glimpse of small fishing boats busy with their catch in the distance as we look through the gnarled limbs and clustered needles of an old pine tree.

§75. Two Famous Plum Trees of Zuiganji, Matsushima

Here we have two views of the famous Red and White Sleeping-Dragon Plums of Zuiganji (Zuigan Temple) on Matsushima. Looking through the temple's central gate toward the close, or inner garden, one sees these two ancient plums. Both are in full bloom. In the first sketch we see the white plum with its famous cast-iron lantern; in the second, the red. They suffuse the whole enclosure with their fragrance.

There is indeed a romantic history! About three hundred years ago, we learn from chronicles of the period, the local feudal lord, Daté Masamune, joined Hotaiko's expeditionary force in Korea. Yet even in the coils of war Masamune was so captivated by the beauty of these two Korean plums that he brought them all the way back with him and planted them in this Zen temple garden.

§76. A Novitiate's Grotto

Over a thousand years ago the well-known priest, Jikaku, after having traveled all over Japan in search of a suitable site, chose this location as the ideal place for training novitiate priests in Zen. Here he and his followers first excavated a cave in which to meditate. Since then generations of disciples and priests have excavated many others. In this sketch we see a characteristic cluster of sculptured Buddhas and engraved Buddhist inscriptions hewn from the native stone between the mouths of several such caves.

§ 77. The Famous Godaido of Matsushima

About thirty miles east of Sendai, largest city of northeastern Japan, lies one of the three major scenic wonders of the nation, Matsushima National Park. It includes within its domain an archipelago of two hundred and eighty islands of all sizes, large and small. Most of these islands are covered with pine, cherry, and maple trees. From the mainland facing the archipelago one sees the wharf and ferryboats that visit these islands teeming with tourists on their way to and fro. In the left foreground on a small island the Godaido still stands in its original form after nine centuries.

§78. Girl Students in Costumes of Their Own Making

A visit to a remarkable rural school is depicted in this sketch. Unlike most girls' schools, this institution is set up to help the daughters of poor farmers prepare themselves for more useful, more abundant lives as wives, mothers, and housekeepers in the large agricultural area surrounding the city of Morioka. Situated in Nakano-Saikawa, a suburb of that city, the Morioka Seikatsu Gakko (school for training girls in homemaking) as this institution is known, enjoys a fine view of Mt. Iwate or Nambu Fuji in the distance. In this school, about one-hundred girls from fourteen to eighteen years of age learn the domestic arts of weaving and sewing, dyeing both fabrics and papers, and, of course, of cooking. In addition to such essential household skills, they are also taught how to sow and harvest in the open fields.

In the sketch we see the girls in their school costumes for field work. Since they make all their own clothes—including the weaving and dyeing of the fabrics—they are setting an example for their less privileged neighbors. For though their costumes follow the traditional patterns in color, texture, and design, they are none the less greatly superior in workmanship to the run-of-the-mill work clothes of most farming folk. In short, the natural beauty of these girls, set off by their own fine flair for combining utility, simplicity, and taste in their costumes, makes one really believe that Japan is still a nation of artists.

§79. Deer Dancers

The *shishi odori* is a popular folk dance in Iwate Prefecture. According to the legend, over a thousand years ago the Priest Kuya lived in a hermitage on a nearby mountainside. Deer used to frisk and play in front of his simple shelter. One day a hunter shot and killed one of these deer. Priest Kuya was so saddened by this loss that he begged the hunter for the pelt of his kill. Later on he asked one of the villagers to dance in this deerskin in memory of the deer.

To this day the farmers around Hanamaki Hot Springs do the *shishi odori*, or deer dance, in the spring at cherry blossom time and in the fall when the maple leaves turn scarlet, the two most popular picnic seasons in Japan.

Deer are traditionally believed to be the messengers of the god of Kasuga Shrine; therefore the costumes of the *shishi odori* dancers all bear the calligraphic motto of Kasuga. In Chinese characters, the motto means "spring day." A piece of white paper dangling from the end of a long bamboo pole attached to the back of each dancer represents the bearded head of a stalk of Japanese pampas grass, symbol of autumn. Eight in each troupe, they dance and cavort in a lively and vigorous manner as they strike large drums suspended from their necks.

§80. Cherry Blossoms at Hirosaki Castle

The accompanying sketch is designed to convey something of the beauty of what has become the finest display of cherry blossoms in all Japan. This magnificent cherry grove encircles Hirosaki Castle, erected in 1611 by Nambu Yoshihiro. Since the castle was surrounded by three moats, the intervening earthworks were tastefully planted with these beautiful cherry trees. Three separate lords were the donors responsible for this large memorial grove, now numbering about five thousand trees in all. The beauty of these aged trees is further enhanced by the skillful planting of pine trees here and there within the grove. The original structure has been largely destroyed by many fires, and today only one portion of the castle proper and one gate remain to remind us of its one-time glory and of the antiquity of these venerable trees.

§81. The View of Nambu Fuji from Hirosaki Castle

Though less renowned than Mt. Fuji, which it resembles in contour, snow-covered Nambu Fuji rising in the clear spring sky above the cherry blossoms surrounding Hirosaki Castle, gives scale and accent to this lovely spring landscape.

§82. View of a Headland, Lake Towada

About a four-hour drive from Aomori Station is Towadako (Lake Towada). The road skirts the Hakkodasan (mountain) as it approaches this lovely lake tucked away in a corner of the Tohoku area, where the boundaries of the Iwate, Aomori, and Akita prefectures converge. The road roughly parallels the Oirasegawa (Oirase River) until it reaches the lake port of Mizunokuchi. Here the traveler boards an excursion boat for a two-hour cruise around the lake. Jutting out into the lake here and there are rocky promontories of brownish lava often rising almost sheer for a thousand feet or more from the lake's surface. Obviously remnants of ancient volcanic eruptions, the decomposed lava of these rocky headlands offers a fertile foothold for all kinds of trees, shrubs, and ferns, including clusters of *kaede* maples, mountain azaleas, *momi* (white fir), *tsuga* (hemlock-spruce), and *katsura* (Japanese Judas tree). From time immemorial, because of their inaccessibility, these forests have probably been left untouched by human hands. A true mountain lake (Towadako's surface is some seven thousand feet above sea level), its surface constantly changes throughout the day. It is especially beautiful during autumn.

§83. A Drizzle at Yuze

Yuze Spa is situated on both banks of the Yoneshirogawa (Yoneshiro River) in the mountains of Akita Prefecture. This resort offers the weary traveler an ideal resting place before continuing his journey. In the accompanying sketch a typical group of farming folk can be seen across the river on their way to work or, perhaps, returning home from the fields—all their outlines softened by a smokelike, misty drizzle. In front of the brownish, distant bank, the verdure of a grove of Japanese cedar seems intensified by the silently falling rain.

§84. Hokkaido University

More than eighty years ago Dr. Clark came from the United States to the then undeveloped island of Hokkaido and established an agricultural college. He remained here year after year, constantly and unselfishly laboring to expand and improve the educational facilities of the college. On its five-hundred-acre campus are many elm trees that he planted years ago. In the sketch we see the little milking shed, built during Dr. Clark's presidency and preserved as a memorial to this man, thanks largely to whose pioneering efforts a modest agricultural college has since grown into the flourishing Hokkaido University of today.

§85. A Bathing Pool

One of the hot spring resorts of Hokkaido is the Jozankei Spa about a two-hour drive from Sapporo. All the hot spring pools of this resort are completely tiled, including the ceilings, walls, and walks. The larger pools vary from fifty to sixty feet in length, and five or six such pools comprise each bathroom unit. The reason for this elaborate arrangement is that each pool is maintained at a different temperature so that the bather can suit his own taste. It is the custom to scrub oneself clean and to take a shower before dipping into these pools, which are constantly being replenished with fresh, hot spring water. While enjoying the water the bather also enjoys the beauty of tropical plants which grow just outside the windows of the bathhouse.

§86. Tarumaegawa Gorge

An hour's drive from Jozankei Spa brings the traveler to the banks of the Tarumaegawa (Tarumae River). After walking some distance downstream he comes abruptly to the brink of the magnificent Tarumaegawa gorge which has been carved out of solid rock by the rushing river. Heavy rainstorms sometimes pour millions of gallons of water into this watershed, uprooting trees and tossing them about like so many chopsticks as they shoot the rapids.

§87. The Hot Spring Vapors of Noboribetsu

Noboribetsu Spa, perhaps the largest in the Far East, is renowned for the abundance and variety of its hot springs as well as for the grand scale of its resort facilities. An immense mountain range called Jigokudani serves as a dramatic backdrop to the setting. The valleys of this range are constantly enveloped in veils of steam from the vapors thrown off by countless hot springs. The favorite time for sightseers to visit this region is in late spring when the ground is still covered with snow.

§88. The Fishing Village of Shiraoi

The entire scene confronting the traveler's eye here in the fishing village of Shiraoi—the sea, the fisherman's shacks, the clouds, and ships at sea—appear to have been painted in grays and blacks. One feels himself to be on the most desolate part of Hokkaido. How wild and lonely it all is! One recalls the Oiwake folk song:

> "The misery that one suffers on a stormy day
>   Makes one resolve once again to quit the   fisherman's life!"

§89. Ainu Fishermen

Gray coldness extends out over the vast expanse of ocean beyond the very horizon here! On the beach the Ainu (Japanese aborigines), fishermen are making ready to launch their boats for the day's catch.

§90. Ezo Fuji on Toyako, Hokkaido

In this sketch we look across serene Toyako (Lake Toya) toward flat-topped Ezo Fuji which commands a panoramic view of the lake. On the lake's mirror-like surface glides an excursion boat. And on the opposite shore nestles the town of Toya against the base of its guardian mountain.

§91. Showa Shinzan, Hokkaido

Naturally enough, spring visits Hokkaido late in the season; yet as the traveler journeys southward from Shiraoi, he enjoys the gradually advancing spring, in the deepening greens of the fields and meadows. As he approaches the newly risen volcano of Showa Shinzan, he sees a continuous pillar of smoke issuing out its crater formed of red-and-black lava. At its foot one finds the inevitable rest-and-souvenir shop catering to sightseers and souvenir-hunters.

§92. Benten Islands, Lake Toya

From our high outlook above Toyako, the pyramidally shaped Benten Islands shining; golden in the sunlight seem to float one above the other as the eye rises. Indeed, the sky is almost cloudless on this resplendent day, save for three solitary cloudlets hovering over these islands like an omen of peace.